Balance Sheet Analysis

Sharma Raj Kumar

Published by Sharma Raj Kumar, 2022.

While every precaution has been taken in the preparation of this book, the publisher assumes no responsibility for errors or omissions, or for damages resulting from the use of the information contained herein.

BALANCE SHEET ANALYSIS

First edition. February 12, 2022.

Copyright © 2022 Sharma Raj Kumar.

ISBN: 979-8201630225

Written by Sharma Raj Kumar.

Table of Contents

BALANCE SHEET ANALYSIS

A guide for investors & bankers

Author's Note

Balance sheet analysis can reveal lot of important information about the company. A user of balance sheet if interpret the figures correctly can safeguard his interests and protect himself against creative accounting practices.

Some of the key importance of balance sheet are

- It is a snapshot of company's assets, liabilities & equity on a given date.
- It is used by management, investors, bankers, & creditors rating agencies to understand the financial health of a company.
- If compared year-on-year basis, it can give indications of company's performance over the years and also the likely trajectory of company's future growth.
- It is the minimum requirement for availing credit facilities from banking system.
- Users can interpret balance sheet to know the liquidity & leverage position of a company.
- It is used by investors to compare with other companies and to find out stocks good for value investing.
- It enables the credit providers to ascertain proper utilization of funds by the company.
- It is used by regulators to ensure regulatory compliances.
- It is used by tax authorities to ascertain tax liabilities on the company.

- It is used by private equity investors, venture capital funds to ascertain value of a company and to acquire stake at appropriate price.
- It is used by top management to ascertain, if the company is moving in right direction or needs some course correction.

The use of balance sheet and its interpretation is different for different user group and thus clarity & accuracy of the numbers used and their classification is very important.

In this book, author has tried to elaborate basic structure of balance sheet along with classification of assets and liabilities of a company. The book provides commonly used tools for interpretation of balance sheet information for use by bankers and investors.

[]

Monu an entrepreneur

Monu a young adult from Hyderabad wishes to start a business. After careful planning he decided to start textile business, though at a much smaller level.

He invested Rs100000/- i.e., a part of his savings to this new venture. This amount invested by him in the business is called **equity** and he became the only **shareholder** of the firm with 100% ownership.

With this investment he purchased five stitching machine and purchased a small shop to start with. These investments in machine & shop are his **long-term assets** & classified as fixed assets.

He approached a bank with his project and requested bank to fund for purchase of cloths, threads, buttons & other material used in manufacturing of garments. These cloths, threads, buttons, which is raw material for the manufacturing of garments is called **inventory** & the finance availed for it from bank is called **short term finance or working capital finance** and is classified under **current liability** as it has to be paid within the operating cycle or maximum one year period.

Monu started the work and used part of raw material for manufacturing of garments. Till the time this raw material is moved from raw material state and finally converted to the goods ready for sale, the goods are called **work in process** and the final goods are called **finished goods**. All three i.e., raw material, work in process & finished goods are part of **inventory**.

After manufacturing the garments, he approached retail & wholesalers for selling of his products, the retails and wholesalers demanded a credit period i.e., a time period for paying the price of the goods purchased from Monu.

This credit extended to retailers and wholesalers by Monu is termed as **trade receivables**. Trade receivables are also known as **sundry debtors**.

Monu sold the goods to these retailers and wholesalers but will receive the amount after an agreed period of time. This period is called **credit period** extended by Monu to retailers & suppliers.

Monu is now in a fix as he will be realizing his money only after an agreed credit period but his business needs money on continuous basis. He again approached his banker for a short-term loan, this loan provided by bank is called **receivable financing** which can be done by way of bill purchase, bill discounted, bill negotiation.

The **trade receivable is classified as current asset** and the short-term finance availed for it from bank is classified as **current liability**. The trade receivable has to be in line with working capital cycle and should be realized within one year or the agreed period, whichever is less.

Monu thought that when he has to extend credit to retailers and wholesalers for selling of his garments, why can't he try to get a credit period from his suppliers i.e., suppliers of cloths, threads, buttons, spare parts etc.

He negotiated with his raw material suppliers and convinced them to provide a credit period. Now Monu is purchasing raw material on credit terms and using it to manufacture the garments but is paying to the suppliers after pre-agreed period at agreed terms and conditions. This credit availed from suppliers is called **Trade Payable** & as it is to be paid by Monu in future date, it will be classified as **current liability**. These trade payables are also known as **sundry creditors**.

Monu was very happy that his business has started but soon he realized that he needs to increase his business & for this he needs to purchase additional machineries and also need to set up a big factory.

He again approached his banker with his plan, bank was happy with performance of Monu's existing project and the re-payment of existing loans. After looking to his past record bank agreed to provide the loan. Bank sanctioned a loan for 5 years tenor. This loan for a period more than one year is known as term loan and **is classified as non-current liability or long-term liability** and the assets acquired by using this loan i.e., machinery is classified under **fixed asset** and **non-current / long term assets**.

The portion of term loan payable within next one year is classified as current liability.

The machineries purchased by Monu has a useful life period of 10 years and Monu needs to make provision towards replacement of these machinery. This provision towards replacement of machinery is termed as **depreciation**.

Depreciation needs to be provided for all fixed assets having useful life excluding land and the rate at which this provision is to be made is termed as **rate of depreciation**.

The Bank's has told Monu to maintain books of accounts in proper formats and as per best accounting standards. These best accounting standards are **International Accounting Standards** or **International financial reporting standards**.

Monu has hired an accountant to keep the books in order and as per best international accounting standards.

The accountant prepared position of all the assets and liabilities of the Monu's firm on a given date. This statement of accounts on a given date describing all the assets and liabilities of a firm is called **Balance Sheet**.

Along with Balance Sheet the accountant also prepared the summary of income and expenses incurred by Monu's firm in a period of last one year. This statement of income and expenses is known as **Profit & Loss Statement**.

The accountant also prepared a statement on movement of cash in the company i.e., a statement indicating flow of cash is know as **cash flow statement**. This is very useful statement as without cash a company will not be able to pay back its short-term expenses / liabilities and will face liquidity shortage.

The business was doing well and now Monu found many of his friends and relatives showing interest in this lucrative business. He agreed to sell a part of company's equity to his friends against a sizable consideration. This transfer of share from Monu to his friend's result into infusion of fresh funds into the business, this fresh infusion of fund is called **equity investment** and resulted in change in **Shareholding Pattern**.

The accountant of Monu's firm has prepared a statement on the movement of share-holding pattern of the firm, this statement reflecting position of share-holdings of a company / firms on a given date and the movement of shareholding during the past one year is termed as **share-holding pattern report**.

BALANCE SHEET ANALYSIS

After this change in shareholding pattern, the key promoters including Monu decided to change the firm from partnership to limited company and listed the company on a stock exchange to raise funds from public in general by issuing part of equity as shares. Now Monu's firm has become a **public limited company** and now the number of shareholders of the company increased from earlier 3-5 close friends and relatives to general public.

The process of money raised from general public by listing company on stock exchange is known as **initial public offering** (IPO). The market for IPO is known as **primary market**. After allotment of share to the public against the amount paid by them, these shares will now trade on stock exchange where anyone can buy or sell it. This market of buying and selling stocks through stock exchanges is known as **secondary market**.

The business has generated a profit of Rs 1cr this year and the board of the company decided to distribute a part of this profit to the equity investors, this distribution of profit to the shareholders is called **dividend**.

The equity shareholders have right on the portion of profit which remained after meeting all expenses and the part of profit retained for future expansion.

A part of profit, the board of the company decided to keep intact for future growth of company. This amount of profit retained in company in comparison to the total profit is known as **retention ratio** & the percentage of profit distributed as dividend is known as **dividend payout ratio**.

After a hard work of 10 years, now Monu's company is a world-famous textile company and has a world-wide recognition. The company is able to attract business on the basis of its reputation and brand. This value generated by company is called **brand value** and this is treated as an **intangible asset** in the balance sheet.

Monu's business has now increased many folds. He decided to acquire a textile unit in Europe to expand his business. Monu acquired European company at a price higher than the fair price of its net assets (assets-liabilities), Monu agreed to pay this higher purchase price because the European company was enjoying a good customer base, reputation, proprietary technology & good customer /employee relations. This value paid over and above the net asset value is termed as **Goodwill** and classified as non-current asset in the balance sheet.

Monu's company now has to issue performance guarantee for securing contracts overseas. This obligation towards performance guarantee or financial guarantee which might crystalize on future date is termed as **contingent liability**.

The contingent liability is any liability which is not certain but might crystalize on a future date. It can be because of legal issues, tax disputes, bank guarantees, Letter of credit, Derivative etc.

Derivative are the financial instruments used to hedge against adverse movement of foreign exchange conversion rate or interest rate or underlying asset price linked to the underlying transaction / security.

BALANCE SHEET ANALYSIS

I hope the basic concept of Balance sheet and classification of assets & liabilities is clear from the above example of Monu's company. Now in next chapter, we will discuss in details the Balance Sheet and the classification of assets and liabilities in the balance sheet.

******

Introduction to Balance Sheet

Balance sheet is a statement of account incorporating assets of a company on a given date and the sources of funding for financing these assets. These sources of funds are classified as debt & equity.

Thus, Balance sheet can also be termed as statement of assets, liabilities & shareholder's equity of a company at a given point of time.

Balance sheet is divided into three basic sections. In a traditional T shaped Balance sheet, the left side is used for incorporating assets owned by a company & right side is used to incorporate liabilities and shareholder's equity which is used to fund these assets.

<table>
<tr><td rowspan="2">Assets
(Current Assets + Non-Current Assets)</td><td>Liabilities
(Current + Non-Current Liabilities)</td></tr>
<tr><td>Net Worth
(Share Capital + Retained Earnings)</td></tr>
</table>

Assets = Liabilities + Shareholders' Equity

Company being a separate legal entity is liable to repay back the shareholder's contribution also at the time of liquidation after meeting all other liabilities. Thus, shareholder's equity is also a liability for the company.

In a normal course of business, a company has to acquire various assets for functioning, these assets can be acquired for use in the short term i.e., for working capital or production purpose like Raw Material, Stores & Spares etc. Similarly, company also needs to acquire fixed assets which are not directly related to the short-term working capital requirement but are essential for the operations of a company example; Plant & Machinery.

Company needs money to acquire these assets, the sources of money and the amount raised is called liabilities. The liabilities can further be classified into debt and equity. Debt is the amount of loan raised by the company and equity is the promoter's contribution.

For Balance Sheet purpose any liability which is due within one year from the date of balance sheet is classified under current liability and any liability due for repayment after one year is classified under non-current liability.

Similarly, current assets are assets which are to be used in a period of one year from the date of balance sheet and generally will have direct relationship with the working capital cycle of a company while non-current assets are generally have a life of more than one year.

Another way of defining Balance Sheet is, it's a statement of sources & uses of fund at a given point of time. The liabilities are the sources of funds and the assets are the uses of fund.

Balance sheet is a very useful statement and companies have to prepare and issue this statement along with Profit & Loss statement for use by investor, regulatory, management & general public.

The authenticity of figures incorporated in Balance Sheet & Profit & Loss statement are of significant importance as various users will take their decisions based on these figures and a false statement or statement hiding crucial aspects of a company can mislead the related parties. Thus, a user of these statements has to learn to interpret these statements so as to safeguard their own interest.

Balance sheet is one of the key parts of financial reports of a company, the other important statements are Profit & Loss Statement, Cash Flow Statement, Directors Report & Auditor's Reports, shareholding pattern & disclosures.

A user should consider all the above before taking any decision or reaching any conclusion.

A standalone Balance sheet rarely gives any major breakthrough, an intelligent user should compare the trends and also consider the other reports i.e., Profit & Loss report, Directors Report, Auditors Reports, before reaching any conclusion. Apart from the above four reports cash flow report is also a very useful tool for investors / users of financial statement.

Balance sheets are also prepared in a vertical format:

			March 2020	March 2019
Assets	Current Assets	4		
	Non-Current Assets	4a		
	Total Assets			
Liabilities	Current Liabilities	5		
	Non-Current Liabilities	5a		
Equity	Share Capital + Reserves & Surplus	6		

You can see that this vertical Balance sheet is in comparative format i.e., enabling user to compare year on year changes in the various heads under assets and liabilities. There is a column containing annexure number. In case of big companies, the Balance sheet will contain multiple annexures, giving breakup of individual assets or liabilities.

A company with subsidiaries will have to prepare Balance sheet as a standalone entity as well as a consolidated Balance Sheet.

Consolidated financial statements are the financial statements of a group in which assets, liabilities, equity, income, expenses & cash flows of the parent company and is subsidiaries are presented as those of a single economic entity.

Significant influence: If an entity holds, directly or indirectly i.e., through subsidiaries etc., 20% or more of the voting power of the investee, it is presumed to have significant influence, unless it can be clearly demonstrated that this is not the case.

Another thumb rule to understand & prepare Balance sheet is

All the money which comes into the company can be classified either Income or Liabilities.

All the money that goes out of the company can be classified either as Expenditure or Assets.

Income & Expenditure will form part of profit & loss statement.

Example;

Raw Material: The money goes out of company & thus it is an Asset.

Loan & Advances availed by the company: The money comes into the company thus it is a Liability.

Interest paid on Loans and Advances raised by the company: Expenditure as money goes out of the company.

Interest received by company: Income as money comes into the company.

BALANCE SHEET ANALYSIS

Now we will understand the classification of different assets, liabilities in the Balance sheet and their interpretations.

Assets

Assets are the uses of funds by a company at a given point of time and can be classified into

- Current Assets
- Non-Current Assets

Assets are items owned by company with the expectation that it will yield financial benefits in future. The benefits can be by way of enhanced revenue, cost reduction or cash generation.

Current Assets

Current Assets are the assets that can be converted into cash within one year. These assets are expected to have high degree of liquidity and can be comfortably consumed, sold or used within one year in normal course of business.

Current assets are used to fund day to day business operations and are used to pay for ongoing operating expenses.

A user of balance sheet has to be careful in assessing the capacity of an asset to be easily liquidated and converted to cash for being classified under Current asset.

Any asset even having a maturity period of less than one year but if illiquid in nature and it is expected that company will face problems in converting it to cash, should not be classified under Current assets.

The components of Current assets are

- Inventory
- Investment in Equity of other companies (held for sale)
- Financial Assets
    - Trade Receivables
    - Cash & Cash Equivalent
    - Bank Balance other than above
    - Finance Receivables
    - Loan & Advances
    - Other Financial Asset
    - Other Investment
- Current tax assets (net)

- Assets classified as held for sale
- Other Current Assets

We will understand each one of the above assets and will find out why it is classified under Current assets.

Inventory

Inventory consists of stock of Raw Material, Finished Goods &
Work in Progress, Stores & Spares, Consumable tools & Goods
in transit.

> **Inventories are assets:**
> Held for sale in the ordinary course of
> business;
> in the process of production for such
> sale;
> or in the form of materials or supplies
> to be consumed in the production

Raw Material: Raw Material is material used in manufacturing the goods and thus a part of production cycle. These are
commodities like Iron, Steel, Plastic, etc which are either in raw
form or in the form of a manufactured parts to be used in production cycle.

Work in Progress: When raw material is moved from
stock to production line for processing and manufacturing of
the goods, the classification of commodity used is changed
from raw material to work in progress.

Finished Goods: The raw material converted to finished
goods but before sale is classified under finished goods category.

Stores, Spares & consumable tools: The stores, spares &
consumable tools which are used directly in connection with
the production of the goods are classified under current inventory.

Good in transit: The finished goods which are not yet sold but are in transit needs to be classified under Inventory. Similarly, the raw material which has been billed though it is in transit and has not reached the company's warehouse will also be classified under inventory.

> International Accounting Standard 2 deals with Inventory.

> Inventory is valued at lower of cost price or net realizable value.
>
> Cost Price: Cost of purchase + Direct expenses linked to bringing the Inventory in present form (Includes; cost of conversion + transport cost)
>
> Net Realizable value: Selling price – All direct expenses linked to sale of good

BALANCE SHEET ANALYSIS

Important Points

- As a user of Balance Sheet, you need to find out the inventories which are not moving. To do this you need to compare the list of inventories between two or more successive periods. Change the non-moving or obsolete inventory classification from current assets to non-current assets.

- Working capital = CA-CL; thus, a high inventory, though not moving will inflate the working capital requirement and the lending bank if ignore ths aspect will end up financing non-moving or obsolete assets which are not current assets.

- Inclusion of obsolete inventory in current assets will distort the financial ratios like current ratio, quick ratio etc and thus will give rosy picture of a company's financial which in actual are not so good.

Investment in Equity (held for sale)

A company invests amount in its subsidiaries, associates and joint ventures & if that investment is kept under the category Held for Sale than it can be classified under current asset.

Shares, debentures and other securities held for sale in the ordinary course of business are disclosed as 'stock-in-trade' under the head current assets.

As a financer, bank normally does not consider this investment under current assets while calculating working capital requirement. Reason being, banks are supposed to fund for the current assets which are actually required for the production purpose i.e., for day to day working of the company and not for its strategic investments.

Banks can fund for such equity investment by the company but not through working capital route.

Further though the investment is categorised as Held for Sale but it is not easy to liquidate the shareholding quickly unless the investee company is a publicly listed entity. The off-market/ private equity deals for sale and purchase of stake in an unlisted company takes a lot of time and efforts.

> Equity investment in associate or subsidiary is to be dealt with in accordance of International Accounting Standard 28, & IFRS-5.

Financial Assets

- Other Investment
- Trade Receivables
- Cash & Cash Equivalent
- Bank Balance other than above
- Finance Receivables
- Loan & Advances
- Other Financial Assets

The basic criteria for categorizing any financial assets under current assets is

- Liquidity
- Maturity

So, if the financial assets are liquid i.e., easily convertible to cash as and when company needs it and its term of investment is less than one year than such assets can be classified under current assets. Further the asset should not be showing any sign of stress other than the normal business risk.

Trade Receivables

In a normal course of business, company's extend credit to wholesalers, retailers. The wholesalers & retailers will receive the goods from company without paying full amount and will get a time period to repay the amount of the goods purchased.

This credit period extended by a company to its wholesalers & retailers is termed as Trade Receivables.

As these are to be received by company, so it is an asset in the books of the company and it will be a liability in the books of the wholesalers & retailers which have availed this facility.

The trade receivable period varies from industry to industry but, in any case, it has to be less than one year (generally 90-180 days) for being eligible to be classified as current assets.

As a user of Balance Sheet, we need to observe whether the trade receivables are paid within the stipulated period or not. If the trade receivable is not paid in the stipulated period than it has to be moved from current assets and classified under non-current assets.

Further a company might also need to write off its trade receivable amount if the prospects of recovery are doubtful.

Trade Receivables are also known as Sundry Debtors.

Trade Receivables is a common tool used to inflate current assets level in a balance sheet by companies seeking higher financing for its working capital requirements.

A prudent banker will find out the trade receivables which are non-current i.e., are not paid in the prescribed period and its prospects of recovery are bleak. They generally exclude these sub-standard trade receivables from their calculation for working capital assessment.

An investor also needs to take care of the asset quality off these trade receivables (though difficult to find) as higher trade receivables inflates current assets thus improving financial ratios.

Cash & Cash Equivalent

Cash is not only physical cash with the company but also the unencumbered balance in the bank accounts of the company. This is the amount which company can withdraw at any point of time without any problem.

Cash Equivalent are the assets which can be quickly converted to cash like investment in freely traded Government Securities, bank deposits which can be prematurely withdrawn etc.

Bank Balance other than above

Apart from Cash & Cash Equivalent, company might also have deposited amount which is earmarked for certain specific purpose, like; margin money deposit for bank guarantee or other bank deposits like fixed deposits etc., The unencumbered /likely to be unencumbered portion of such amount can also be included in current assets depending upon their liquidity and maturity profile.

Finance Receivables

Any other short term account receivable which is not directly linked with trade can be classified as finance receivable. It can be receivables on account of certain credit extended to a party. It has to be again bifurcated between current & non-current finance receivables.

Loans & Advances

A company extends loans and advances to its subsidiaries, associates, dealers, wholesalers, retailers, customers. All these loans & advances extended by company are an asset in the book of the company. The part of loans & advances which is recoverable within one year, and where the loans and advances are not showing any sign of problem, are classified under current assets.

If the dues are not paid on time, then the company will have to move these assets from current asset to non-current asset category and might also have to write it off, if chances of recovery are bleak.

In case of Loans & Advances given by company for longer tenor, only repayments due for realization on standard assets within one year are to be considered under Current Assets

Standard Asset is one which does not disclose any problems, and which does not carry more than normal risk attached to the business.

Other Financial Assets

Other Financial assets can include derivatives, accrued interest on loans and advances, Government grants receivable, short term deposits with financial institutes (other than those included above), recovery from suppliers, lease receivable etc.

International Accounting Standard 39 deals with financial instruments.

Current tax assets (net)

Company's pay advance tax and at the time of preparation of Balance sheet, if the tax paid is higher than the actual tax to be paid, than the difference between these two will be an asset for the company and company can classify it under current / non-current asset depending upon the probable date of realization of refund of this tax.

It has to be classified separately as the time period of its realization is not certain and thus if included in other heads like Cash & Cash equivalent or finance receivable, it will not give true picture for assessment of working capital requirement.

> International Accounting Standard 12 deals with treatment of Income tax in financial statements.

Non-Current Assets

Non-Current Assets are all the assets which are not eligible to be classified as current assets. The key characteristics of non-current assets are

- Financial assets whose realisability and convertibility to cash within one year is doubtful.
- Fixed Assets (Plant & Machinery)
- Intangible assets like goodwill, brand value etc.
- Long term loans and advances extended by company, repayment of which will fall after one year.
- Tax credits, which are deferred.
- Equity investment which is not categorized as held for trading or held for sale.
- Trade receivable not likely to be realized in a year's time or which are remain unpaid despite of completion of prescribed credit period.
- Capital work in progress

Financial Assets

A financial asset is any asset that is;

- Cash (To be classified as current asset)
- An equity instrument of another entity
- A contractual right

✓ To receive cash or another finance asset from another entity or

✓ To exchange financial asset or financial liabilities with another entity under conditions that are favourable to the company

In case of financial assets the convertibility to cash and maturity profile is an important metrics for classification into current or non-current assets.

International accounting standard 32 defines financial assets and explains its treatment in balance sheet.

Fixed Assets

A company needs to invest in various fixed assets which though are not directly linked to the production process but are essential for the production process and the survival of the company e.g., Land, Machinery, Building, Vehicle, Office Space etc.

The cost of an item of property, plant and machinery shall be recognised as an asset only if,

- It is probable that future economic benefits associated with the asset will flow to the entity.
- The cost of the item can be measured reliably.

Items such as spare part, stand-by equipment's etc, if does not meet above conditions than they are classified as inventory instead of classifying under fixed assets or are written off.

Acquiring fixed assets require large outlay of funds and the assets will have a longer life than the life of a current asset like Raw Material etc. Further the conversion of these assets to cash will have lots of challenges and it cannot be done quickly.

> International accounting standard 16 deals with accounting of Property, Plant & Machinery.

Out of these fixed assets, the assets whose value deteriorate with time example machinery will attract depreciation.

Land does not attract depreciation as it does not need to be replaced after a given time period. Land is considered to have infinite useful life.

> Depreciation is the systematic allocation of depreciable amount of an asset over its useful life. Two most common methods of calculating depreciation are straight line method & written down method.

Nearly all fixed assets except land have useful life and after which they no longer contribute to the revenue generation of the company and are need to be replaced.

During this useful life period the fixed assets are depreciated by certain percentage to reduce their worth and at last only salvage value will remain.

Only in case of land which are used to extract certain natural resources are accounted for depreciation using depletion method as the natural resources will not last for long and thus depreciation needs to be provided for.

Intangible Assets

These are non-physical assets with long useful period. The future benefit of intangible assets is uncertain and thus valuation of these assets is problematic. Some of the intangible assets commonly find place in Balance Sheet are

- Goodwill
- Trademark
- Patents & Copyrights
- Brand
- Licensing agreements
- Computer Software & Internet Domain
- Blueprints, Medical Records, Manuscripts

The value of Intangible asset depends upon its use in the future and thus it's difficult to ascertain its correct value and it mostly depends upon perception.

Expenditure for an intangible item is recognised as an expense, unless the item meets following condition

1. It has future economic benefit
2. Its cost can be reliably measured.

If above conditions are met then this intangible item can be classified as intangible asset in Balance Sheet.

In Balance Sheet, Intangible assets are listed as asset only if they are acquired and have identifiable value and useful lifespan that can be amortized. It is very difficult to ascertain the value of internally generated intangible asset like brand, good-will etc.

A user of balance sheet needs to ascertain importance of intangible assets in the future growth of the company. Example: A strong & popular brand name can generate future sales and thus needs to be recognized.

International Accounting Standard 38 deals with Intangible Assets.

A Balance Sheet user has to be very careful while taking intangible asset into consideration. It has been seen that value of Intangible assets falls very quickly and significantly if things go wrong.

Deferred Tax Credits

Company sometimes prepay or overpay taxes. The portion of tax which is to be refunded by the tax authority or provide a benefit at some point of time in future is treated as deferred tax credit.

One reason for deferred tax credit can be change in accounting policy or tax laws resulting in tax relief on the prepaid component.

Carryover of losses is also classified as deferred tax asset as it is used to reduces the taxable income in the subsequent years.

Long term Loans & Advances

The amount of loans and advances extended by the company, which falls due after one year are treated as long term loans and advances and are classified under non-current assets.

The portion of standard long-term loans and advances extended by the company, which falls due for recovery within one year is classified under current assets.

Equity Investment

Equity Investment made by company into stocks of subsidiary, associates or other companies with the intention to hold it beyond one year is treated as non-current assets.

An equity investment can only be classified as current asset when it is classified under "held for trading" or "held for sale" segment and there is no major hurdle in disposing of the equity in market within one year.

> International Accounting Standard 28 deals with Investment in Associates & Joint Ventures

Long term trade receivables

We have seen previously that the trade receivables which are in standard category i.e., there is no major risk other than the normal business risk is associated with their realization within one year or the working capital cycle period, are classified under current assets.

Out of these trade receivables, some of the receivables might not be realized on time than such receivables are to be classified under non-current assets.

Similarly, if the periodicity attached to trade receivables is of greater than one year than these receivables are to invariably classified under non-current assets.

This bifurcation is very important, and as a user of Balance sheet, you need to be careful that the unrealized or substandard trade receivables are segregated from the standard trade receivables and are classified either under non-current assets or are written off.

Bank's does not finance sub-standard receivables & thus it become important for a credit analyst to segregate standard and sub-standard receivables and then treat them accordingly.

Capital work in progress

There may be cases, when at the time of preparing Balance sheet, some of the capital work is under progress. Such work needs to be classified under non-current assets under the head Capital work in progress.

The cost being incurred on such assets cannot be recognized as an operating asset until they are ready to use.

Liabilities

Liabilities are the sources of funds for a company. These sources can be either debt or equity. Company being a separate entity, has to raise money either by way of loans & advances or through equity participation.

Equity is also a liability for the company. At the time of liquidation of the company, company will have to repay back the money raised from different stake holder by sale of its assets. In last after settling all dues, if anything is left, that will be distributed to the equity shareholder.

Thus, liabilities can be classified as;

- Current Liabilities.
- Non-Current Liabilities.
- Equity

We will discuss equity in next chapter and will focus on Current & Non-Current Liabilities in this chapter.

Current Liabilities

Current liabilities are short term financial obligation of a company payable within a period of one year from the date of balance sheet or within the normal operating cycle.

Current liabilities are usually settled using current assets. It is thus very important to observe the position of Current Assets via a vis Current Liabilities.

> **Operating Cycle**
> 1. Raw Material Purchase (Cash or Credit-Sundry Creditor)
> 2. Work in Progress
> 3. Finished Goods
> 4. Sales (Cash or Credit -Sundry Debtors)
> 5. Debt Collection from Sundry Debtors
> 6. Cash realization & Repayment to Sundry Creditors
> 7. Back to Step 1

If the short-term Assets are inadequate to meet the short-term Liabilities, then the company might come under financial stress because it is not always easy to realize money by selling non-current assets and repay back the current liabilities. To overcome this situation, analyst consider various financial ratios like Current Ratio, Quick Ratio or Acid-Test Ratio, to examine the liquidity position of the company.

It can be seen from the above operating cycle that on one side of the balance sheet where Sundry Creditors adds value to business by extending credit period on purchase of raw material or inventory thus improving cash flow for the company, Company also has to extend credit period to purchasers to remain competitive in market.

Both trade receivables (Sundry Debtors-Current Assets) & trade payables (Sundry Creditors-Current Liabilities) are important for the company. The efficient management of both of these is important for a company to remain liquid.

Company should try to increase the trade payable period but at the same time should keep trade receivable period as short as possible to improve its cash flows.

A company enjoying higher sundry creditor period and lower sundry debtor period in comparison to other companies, most likely be working in a niche area and enjoying market dominance.

Bank's fund this operating cycle by way of working capital finance.

Working Capital Gap = Current Asset- Current Liability

The excess portion of current assets for which the short-term sources are not available are funded by the bank's using working capital assessment.

Generally, 75% of this working capital gap is funded by bank finance and remaining 25% is bring in by promoters as equity participation (margin money).

This ratio of 3:1 can change depending on the project and the risk involved.

Current Liabilities can be classified under following heads;

- Short term borrowings
- Trade Payables
- Provisions
- Current tax Liabilities

BALANCE SHEET ANALYSIS

- Other current Liabilities

Short term Borrowings

Loans and advances availed by the company to meet short term financial requirements i.e., related to procurement of raw material or related to working capital cycle is classified as current liabilities.

Generally, these loans are payable on demand and have to be repaid from the sales proceeds of the goods manufactured and sold by the company.

As these loans are availed for working capital purpose thus, its maturity will be in line with operating cycle and in general should be less than one year.

Apart from the loans and advances availed for working capital purpose, the portion of longer-term loans payable within one year from the date of balance sheet is also classified under current liabilities.

The short-term borrowing can be by way of cash credit for working capital, demand loans, invoice financing, factoring, commercial papers etc.

The bifurcation of borrowings from banking sector and non-banking sector needs to be obtained to ascertain outside bank borrowings.

> Commercial paper is an unsecured short-term money market instrument issued by corporates to raise short term funds from markets. Commercial papers are raised for tenors ranging from 7days to 365 days.

Trade Payables

Company's purchase raw material and other inventory on credit from its suppliers, these credits are generally in line with the working capital cycle and are to be repaid from the sales proceeds.

Trade payables generally are to be paid within one years and are classified under Current Liabilities. In case if trade payables are not payable within one year than it can be classified as long-term liabilities. Longer term liabilities will also have interest payments associated with it thus these long-term trade payables are normally classifying as long-term debt/ borrowings.

As against trade receivables, there is no question of writing off trade payables or classifying it under sub-standard category as these are liabilities to be paid by the company and thus under prudent accounting practice, we have to assume that company will be paying all its dues in the normal course of business.

Provisions

Companies have to make provisions towards their bad debts i.e., loans and advances / trade receivables, extended by the company where the chances of recovery are bleak.

Company has to make provision towards writing off these sub-standard investments or debts.

Similarly, companies can make provisions towards the future liabilities which are likely to materialize. If company is of the view that outflow is not probable, then it will classify the liability under contingent liability.

> International Accounting Standard 37 deals with accounting for and disclosure of provisions, contingent liabilities and contingent assets.

Other current liabilities

Any other liabilities, which are payable within one year are classified under current liabilities, such as;

- Dividend payable
- Other account payables
- Accrued Expenses
- Accrued Interest

Non-Current Liabilities

Non-Current Liabilities i.e., the financial liabilities which are not due within one year but will arise after one year are classified under non-current liabilities.

- Financial liabilities
- Provisions
- Deferred tax liabilities
- Other non-current liabilities

Non-current liabilities are long term sources of funds and thus used to fund long term assets. It is important for a user of balance sheet to ascertain if company is in a position to generate future cash flows for repayment of these long-term liabilities.

Users of balance sheet ascertain leverage position by comparing long term liabilities with the equity capital.

A company with very high leverage will be open to significant risk of change in economic scenario and a change in one of the variables (e.g., interest rate, sales, fixed cost, variable cost, bad-debts etc.) can lead to severe stress on the cash flows of the bank.

Financial Liabilities

Financial liabilities can be on account of borrowings, lease liabilities, bond or debenture payments, deferred revenue & other financial obligations.

Loans and advances payable after one year are classified under non-current liabilities. It includes bank borrowings as well as borrowings from other parties.

Further borrowings can be by way of term loans, non-convertible debentures or bonds etc.

The classification of borrowings from banking & non-banking is important to ascertain the outside bank borrowings.

Deferred revenue (unearned revenue) is the payment received by company from a customer before the product or service has been delivered. Under accrual accounting, the revenue recognition process has not completed thus the **deferred revenue is treated as liability** in the balance sheet.

Under accrual accounting, revenue is only recognized as earned when money is received from a buyer, and the goods or services are delivered to the buyer.

> Debentures are long term instruments issued by corporates to raise fund from the market.
> Convertible debentures can be converted to equity shares of the issuing company on due date while non-convertible debentures cannot be converted to equity share of the company.

The debt raised by companies through non-convertible debentures should be treated in line with term loan irrespective of whether the company has coupon payment obligations on the NCD or not.

Convertible debentures are also classified as financial liabilities under non-current liabilities in the balance sheet till the holder has not exercised his right to convert it into equity but needs to be clearly mentioned under the head convertible debentures.

The right to get them converted to equity will have to be considered at the time of calculating diluted Earnings per share (EPS).

Provisions

If the provisions are for liabilities maturing beyond one year than, such provision needs to be classified under non-current liabilities.

Provisions can include

- Employee benefit Obligations
- Product warranty
- Legal & Product liability
- Provision for residual risk
- Environmental liability
- Any other provisions.

The following criteria must be met in order to recognize a provision (as per IFRS)

An entity has a current obligation arising from past events

It is probable that an outflow of funds will occur on account of such obligation in future.

The amount of obligation can be estimated with reasonable accuracy.

Deferred tax liabilities

A deferred tax liability is created when there is temporary difference between actual tax and tax paid / provided for in books.

It is important for a user of balance sheet to understand the causes of such difference in tax assessment. A user of balance sheet also needs to understand the impact of such deferred tax liabilities on the future operations / financial position of the company.

An increase in deferred tax liability is a source of income for company as company has not paid this amount to the tax authority and thus this amount is available for the company (though temporarily).

It might be on account of company not able to generate enough cash from its operations and thus trying to shift their liabilities.

A user of balance sheet needs to observe the trends in deferred tax liability and assets. An increasing deferred tax liability could signal that the company is capital intensive, reason being, a new capital asset comes with accelerated tax depreciation that is larger than decelerating depreciation of older assets.

Other non-current liabilities

Any other liabilities that can be ascertained with reasonable accuracy and not falling due within next one year can be classified under the head "Other non-current liabilities".

Equity

Equity is the permanent capital in the business. This belongs to the shareholders, promoters. It is the value to be returned to the shareholder at the time of liquidation of the company after payment of all other debts.

Shareholder's equity=Total Assets – Total Liabilities

It comprises of companies share capital + retained earnings.

Equity is the capital raised by company from promoters, investors to fund companies' operations. As against debt, there is no obligation on company to pay any interest to the shareholder on the amount invested.

Company will have to distribute dividend out of the net profit generated after retaining required portion of net profit for future use.

Company is again not under any legal obligation to declare and distribute dividend every year. Company can retain the profit generated for future use by the company. Further dividend will have to distributed only out of profit generated and a loss-making company will not distribute any dividend.

As an investor, we should look for companies paying regular dividend as it indicates financial discipline. There should be reasonable reasons for company not paying dividend despite of earning profits.

A growth-oriented company generally retain a sizable portion of profit for future expansion or debt reduction as against a established company which generally choose to distribute dividends at a higher rate.

In either way the investors should get benefited either by receiving a part of profit as dividend or by appreciation of share price on account of growth of the company.

As a user of balance sheet, we need to look for uniformity in the principals of accounting adopted by the company and their alignment with the international best practices as illustrated by international accounting standards.

Ramu a Banker

For further expansion of business Monu (now CEO of his company) decided to avail finance from another banker. This movement from only one banker to more than one banker is termed as multiple banking arrangement.

Monu approached Ramu a Banker to avail finance for his textile project. Ramu shared a checklist with Monu and advised him to submit the required papers.

The checklist

a) Existing Bank account statement
b) NOC from existing Bankers
c) Balance Sheet
d) Profit & Loss Statement
e) Cash Flow Statement
f) Memorandum of Association
g) Article of Association
h) Project Report
i) KYC details of key management, etc.

Monu's got all the papers prepared and submitted the same to Ramu. Ramu now has to take a decision to sanction or reject Monu's application.

To ascertain the present position and growth prospects of the company, Ramu is going to analyze the company's balance sheet.

To check the capability of Monu's company to meet its short-term debt obligation, Ramu divided current assets of the company by current liabilities. This ratio of Current Asset to Current Liability is known as **Current Ratio**.

Ramu realized that the current ratio obtained from a standalone balance sheet does not reflect true picture of the company's financial soundness and thus he decided to work out current ratio for past 3-5 years to see the trend. This is known as **trend analysis** and it is one of the most important aspect in analysis of financial statement.

Ramu is now satisfied with the current ratio position and the movement in current ratio over the years. He now decided to check the current ratio of Monu's company with current ratio of other textile companies of similar size.

This comparison of financial position of a company with other companies of similar segment is known as **Peer group comparison** and it is a very useful tool in understanding the position of company's performance in comparison to the average performance of other companies in the similar segment.

After satisfying with short term financial position of the company, Ramu thought, what would happen to the company in case it is not able to sell its inventory on time for meeting its current liability?

With this thought in his mind, he worked out another ratio by taking current assets which are either cash or cash equivalent only (i.e., subtracting inventory from the current assets) and divided it by current liability. This new ratio is known as **Quick Ratio.**

Ramu now decided to check how quickly the company is able to convert its Raw Material to Cash i.e., completes the **operating cycle**. This is very important, as a longer operating cycle might result in cash crunch. Also, Ramu might end up financing obsolete inventory.

Operating cycle

Raw Material- Work in Process- Finished Goods- Credit Sales- Sales Realization – Cash- Raw Material Purchase.

Ramu compared the operating cycle of Monu's company with the average operating cycle of other companies in the sector and got satisfied with the time taken by Monu's company in converting Raw Material to cash.

To find our working capital requirement of the company, Ramu decided to subtract current liabilities from current assets. By doing this Ramu got the amount of current assets which are not funded by current liabilities, i.e., at present either long term liabilities are used to fund these current assets or equity is used to fund these assets.

This surplus of current assets over current liability is known as **working capital gap**.

This working capital gap is to be funded by bank's finance by way of short-term loans also known as **working capital finance** & margin money from the promoter by way of equity infusion.

Ramu realized that the Monu's company is selling its goods both on cash as well as on credit but the realization of credit sales is not proper and there is a huge amount shown under trade receivables heading under current assets in the balance sheet.

Ramu decided to find out the average period taken by Monu's company to realize its trade receivables or commonly known as **collection period**. For this he divided the outstanding trade receivable in the balance sheet (if possible, we should take average outstanding) by the total credit sales in the year and multiplied it by 365 days. By doing this Ramu got the average number of days required by Monu's company to collect the receivables.

He compares this with industry average and found it to be on higher side. Further Ramu also observed that this collection period is increasing over the years. Ramu noted this observation for further cross checking with Monu subsequently.

A higher collection period indicates company's inefficiency in recovery of dues or lack of demand for company's products in the market. This will have adverse impact on the company liquidity position. Further a banker is not supposed to finance obsolete receivables, company will have to write-off these from its balance sheet.

Ramu's attention now moved on to the **trade payables payment period**. To arrive at trade payable payment period, he divided the average outstanding trade payable by credit purchase and multiplied it by 365.

Ramu again got a number which is much higher than the average number of trade payables period for the other industries in the similar sector.

Though higher trade payable period indicates better liquidity position for the company but it also indicates the company is defaulting in payment to its suppliers. The other interpretation of such higher period can be

- The suppliers might discontinue credit sales to Monu's company in future due to loss of creditworthiness by Monu's company.
- Monu's company is facing delay in its realizations

thus not having sufficient money to pay back to its suppliers.

- Non availability of cash.
- Monu's company is enjoying market dominance and thus able to purchase raw material on easy credit terms.

Ramu's attention now moved towards Inventory level. He compares the inventory level of last three years and found it to be satisfactory and also in line with the industry levels.

Being a prudent analyst, he decided to go into the details of inventory list and asked Monu to arrange for **stock statements** for the past 6 months. This will help him to find out any obsolete inventory added in the inventory list by company.

Further, he decided to work into **inventory turnover ratio** to find out how quickly inventory are converted to sales. For this he divided cost of sales by average inventory. This gives him the number of times inventory is rotated in an accounting period. The higher the ratio the better will be the profitability and performance of the company.

A low inventory turnover is generally due to lower sales, obsolescence, low demand of company's product, lack of marketing and distribution efforts and overstocking.

Cost of sales, represents the actual cost of material and other expenses incurred in manufacturing the goods. It excludes indirect costs like marketing, distribution costs.

After satisfying with the short term financial of the company, now Ramu decided to check the long-term financial position of the company.

He decided to check the **financial leverage** position of the company by dividing total debt (interest bearing liability) of the company by equity shareholding (i.e., promoters' contribution).

This ratio of Total **Debt to Equity** is also known as **Gearing Ratio**.

This ratio indicates the portion of Monu's interest in the company, a very high gearing ratio indicates that promoter's stake in the company is very low and in case of first sign of trouble, the promoters / key shareholders might not be interested in saving the company.

Now its turn to check whether company is capable to generate enough revenue to meet its payment obligations arising after Ramu decides to extend fresh loans to the company. With this in mind Ramu divided the net operating income by total debt to be serviced in a given period.

The net operating income is the gross income before subtracting, interest expenses and the total debt to be services is interest + principal portion of the debt.

This ratio is known as **Debt Service Coverage Ratio** and is one of the key ratios used in determining financing for a long-term project.

In next chapter, we will discuss in details, the financial ratios used in interpretation of balance sheet.

******

BALANCE SHEET ANALYSIS

93

Analysis of Balance Sheet - Banker

Balance sheet is a very useful financial statement prepared and provided by company to the user group. It is very important for user of balance sheet to understand the figures and find out their importance.

By using certain ratios, investors and analyst can interpret the financial soundness of the company to a reasonable extend. The comparative data over past few years will enable the investors and analyst to form a view on the financial trends of the company, which in turn can help to ascertain the future prospects of the company.

In this chapter, we will discuss some of the key financial ratios used by credit providers or bankers in analysis of balance sheet.

Balance Sheet and Profit & Loss Statement statements are used to work out these ratios.

For understanding financial position of a company, a user has to ascertain trends in the ratios over time.

Using balance sheet ratios, an investor can compare financial position and performance of different companies in similar industry and can take calculated decision towards investing their hard-earned money.

Ratios from creditors perspective can be grouped into different segments i.e.

Liquidity Ratios –

- Current ratio,
- Quick Ratio,

- Inventory turnover ratio.

Solvency Ratios-

- debt to asset ratio,
- debt to equity ratio.

Efficiency Ratios-

- account receivable turnover,
- fixed asset turnover ratio.

We will use balance sheet of a public listed company for understanding key financial ratios.

BALANCE SHEET ANALYSIS

		31 March 2020	31 March 2019
I. ASSETS			
(1) NON-CURRENT ASSETS			
(a) Property, plant and equipment	3	77882.85	72619.86
(b) Capital work-in-progress		8599.56	8538.17
(c) Right of use assets	4	6275.34	
(d) Goodwill	5	777.06	747.87
(e) Other intangible assets	6 (a)	42171.91	37866.74
(f) Intangible assets under development	6 (b)	27022.73	23345.67
(g) Investment in equity accounted investees	9	4418.88	4743.38
(h) Financial assets:			
(i) Other investments	10	1028.05	1497.51
(ii) Finance receivables	18	16833.77	22073.17
(iii) Loans and advances	12	782.76	407.42
(iv) Other financial assets	13	4749.57	2899.18
(i) Deferred tax assets (net)	22	5457.90	5151.11
(j) Non-current tax assets (net)		1152.05	1024.56
(k) Other non-current assets	20	9381.67	2938.73
		201934.01	**183763.37**
(2) CURRENT ASSETS			
(a) Inventories	14	37456.98	39013.72
(b) Investment in equity accounted investees (held for sale)	9 (c)		591.50
(c) Financial assets:			
(i) Other investments	11	10861.54	8984.33
(ii) Trade receivables	15	11172.69	18996.17
(iii) Cash and cash equivalents	16	18467.80	21559.80
(iv) Bank balances other than (iii) above	17	15259.17	11089.02
(v) Finance receivables	18	14245.30	13551.52
(vi) Loans and advances	12	935.25	3268.70
(vii) Other financial assets	13	4586.48	3211.56
(d) Current tax assets (net)		142.80	184.37
(e) Assets classified as held-for-sale	47 (a)	196.43	167.24
(f) Other current assets	21	6264.91	6862.22
		119587.28	**123431.16**
TOTAL ASSETS		**322121.26**	**307194.53**
II. EQUITY AND LIABILITIES			
EQUITY			
(a) Equity share capital	23	719.54	679.22
(b) Other equity	24	62358.99	59500.34
Equity attributable to owners of company		**63078.53**	**60179.56**
Non-controlling interests		813.56	523.06
		63892.09	**60702.62**
LIABILITIES			
(1) NON-CURRENT LIABILITIES			
(a) Financial liabilities:			
(i) Borrowings	26	83315.62	70817.50
(ii) Lease liabilities		5162.94	356.17
(iii) Other financial liabilities	28	3858.48	2792.71
(b) Provisions	30	14736.69	11854.85
(c) Deferred tax liabilities (net)	22	1941.87	1491.04
(d) Other non-current liabilities	31	8759.52	13922.21
		117778.12	**101034.48**
(2) CURRENT LIABILITIES			
(a) Financial liabilities:			
(i) Borrowings	27	16362.53	20150.26
(ii) Lease liabilities		814.36	17.30
(iii) Trade payables			
(a) Total outstanding dues of micro and small enterprises		109.75	130.69
(b) Total outstanding dues of creditors other than micro and small enterprises		63517.13	68352.84
(iv) Acceptances		2771.33	3177.14
(v) Other financial liabilities	29	36544.00	32838.35
(b) Provisions	30	10329.04	10190.75
(c) Current tax liabilities (net)		1040.14	1017.64
(d) Other current liabilities	32	8965.95	5546.46
		140454.05	**145457.43**
TOTAL EQUITY AND LIABILITIES		**322121.26**	**307194.53**

Liquidity Ratios

Liquidity ratios are used to ascertain the financial position of a company for payment of short-term debts & obligations.

Current Ratio

Current ratio is balance sheet ratio used to measure company's ability to pay short term liabilities by using short term assets.

$$\text{Current Ratio} = \frac{\text{Current Assets}}{\text{Current Liabilities}}$$

A higher current ratio, indicates better financial position of a company. But a very high current ratio in comparison to the other companies in the similar industry or over the past trend indicates either

- Inventory (Current Assets) are not getting sold or higher than normal level of inventory is accumulated.
- Trade Receivables are not getting realized on time signalling stress in the sector and increasing bad debts for the company.
- Company is using cash in place of bank borrowings for business resulting in lower liabilities. It can reflect lack of strength to raise funds from banks.
- A very low current liability in comparison to current asset, though indicate a sound financial position but can also indicate, company's inability to raise funds & increase cash flow through higher trade payables or short-term borrowings.
- Only a strong and reputed company can enjoy higher trade payable period. It is very important for a company to keep financial discipline in timely payment of trade payables.

A very low current ratio indicates company is not able to pay its short-term liabilities from its short-term assets. In such scenario, company might be forced to liquidate its long-term assets to get rid of the short-term financial liabilities.

The reasons for low current ratio can be

- Diversion of fund i.e., funds meant for short term purpose are used for long term purpose. Example: Short term borrowings raised for purchase and processing of inventories are used for purchase of long-term asset like machinery.
- Siphoning of fund i.e., funds are not used in business but are used by company for activity not directly related to the purpose and business for which it is raised.
- Delay in trade payables indicating cash crunch.

It becomes very important for investors and analysts to ascertain that company is classifying current assets and current liabilities in line with the international accounting standards, because a wrong classification can result into wrong interpretation of the financial ratio and thus it will be misguiding.

Lending bank generally have their own models for classification of assets and liabilities into current assets and current liabilities and check each and every item on the balance sheet for its proper classification.

In case of the sample Balance Sheet the current ratio is;

BALANCE SHEET ANALYSIS

	Current Assets	Current Liabilities	Current Ratio
FY 2020	119587	140454	0.85
FY 2019	123431	145457	0.84

The current liabilities position of the company is higher in comparison to the current assets and thus in a normal assessment the financial position of the company might seems to be not comfortable.

This is the reason we have to go beyond the figures and need to look into each and every aspect of the balance sheet. In this scenario, a user of balance sheet needs to check the trend as it might be a temporary phenomenon. Generally, a ratio of 1 and above is treated as good.

If we compare YOY position than, the liquidity position of the company is nearly unchanged or increased only by a fraction. But it can be seen that the improvement in the ratio is not on account of increase in current assets, but it is on account of reduction in both current assets and current liabilities. It can be interpreted as slowdown in activity of the company. A user of balance sheet needs to look into other financial indicators also to form a view on the company.

It is very important to know the industry average to have a better view of the lower current ratio.

Quick Ratio

Quick ratio is a more conservative ratio than current ratio and includes only cash and cash equivalent in current assets.

$$\text{Quick Ratio} = \frac{\text{Cash \& Cash Eqv. + Account Receivable + Marketable Securities}}{\text{Current Liabilities}}$$

We can also write Quick ratio as

$$\text{Quick Ratio} = \frac{\text{Current Assets - Inventory}}{\text{Current Liabilities}}$$

Inventories are removed from current assets because it's difficult to convert inventories to cash quickly in case of need.

	Current Assets - Inventory	Current Liabilities	Quick Ratio
FY 2020	82130	140454	0.58
FY 2019	84417	145457	0.58

Here also the quick ratio is not showing strength and an analyst need to look into the balance sheet annexures to find out reasons for such higher level of current liabilities in comparison to current assets.

Solvency Ratio

Solvency ratio is used to ascertain the company's capability to meet its long-term debt obligations. It indicates the company's cash flow position for repayment of long-term liabilities.

It also indicates the financial leverage position of the company. Excess leverage will make things difficult for the company with slight change in variables impacting the cash flow like adverse interest rate movement.

Debt to Asset Ratio

Debt to asset is used to find the financial leverage position of a company. It indicates the dependence of company on debt vs equity or for every Rs100 investment by promoters/ shareholder how much is the leverage has been taken by availing debt.

The formula for debt to asset ratio is

$$\text{Debt to Asset Ratio} = \frac{\text{Total Liabilities (CL + TL)}}{\text{Total Assets}}$$

As the name suggest the total of debt liabilities needs to be taken into consideration and not the equity portion.

	CL+TL	Total Asset	Debt /Asset
FY 2020	258229	322121	80.16%
FY 2019	246491	307194	80.23%

The ratio indicates the percentage of debt company uses to finance its operations. In the above case the company is using 80.16% of debt to fund its operations. Thus only 19.84% of the company's assets are funded by equity.

A financer will generally look for lower debt to asset ratio because with lower debt to asset ratio the equity participation will be higher thus giving additional cushion to financiers if the firm goes bankrupt. A company with higher debt to asset ratio will be at risk in case of rising interest rate scenario (in case of loan linked to floating rate benchmark).

While comparing with peer group, user need to be careful that the numerator is taken as CL +TL in case of all the companies because some users use only long-term debt in numerators instead of total debt.

In some cases, users of balance sheet will use only financial borrowings portion from current and term liability to calculate total debt instead of total current and term liabilities and also ignore intangible assets while calculating total assets.

	Short + Long term Borrowing	Total Asset - intangibles	Debt /Asset
FY 2020	99678	252149	39.53%
FY 2019	90967	245234	37.09%

It can be seen that with slight change in the interpretation of balance sheet figures, the ratio got distorted and now the position of debt to asset ratio looks much more positive.

In my opinion, a user of balance sheet particularly a creditor needs to be conservative and thus first method of arriving at debt to asset ratio should be more useful.

Debt to equity ratio

This ratio is used to ascertain a company's financial leverage. It is also known as gearing ratio. It indicates the degree to which a company is using its own fund (equity) for financing operations vs through debt. It also indicates the capability of shareholders to cover all outstanding debt in the event of slowdown of business.

$$\text{Debt to Equity Ratio} = \frac{\text{Total Liabilities}}{\text{Shareholder's Equity}}$$

Higher debt to equity ratio indicates higher dependence on debt for funding the operations of the company. This is perceived as a risky position from creditors view.

In a balance sheet

Assets = Liabilities + Shareholder's equity

It means the assets are either funded by liabilities (debt) or by equity (promoters' contribution). The higher the equity portion the lower is the risk perceived by the creditors.

A company can generate higher returns to its shareholders by increasing financial leveraging and availing higher amount of debt to fund the growth. But in such scenario the company will be at greater risk as the interest burden will also increase and with a change in economic scenario this increased burden of debt repayment can make things worse for the company, resulting in decline in share value.

	Total Liabilities	Shareholders' equity	D/E Ratio
FY 2020	258229	63078	4.094
FY 2019	246491	60179	4.096

From above example, we can see that the company has taken four times financial leverage. This also indicates that the promoter's contribution is approx. 20% in the company's assets (1/5).

In some cases, analyst instead of taking entire liabilities as debt, takes only long-term liabilities into consideration for working out debt to equity ratio. Reason for this can be: short term debts are part of operating cycle and are thus will be repaid at the end of operating cycle from sales proceeds i.e., in a period of one year and thus such short-term debt is comparatively less risky than long term debt.

	Long term liabilities	Shareholders' equity	D/E Ratio
FY 2020	117775	63078	1.87
FY 2019	101034	60179	1.68

The third way to calculate debt to equity ratio is to consider only borrowings as debt and ignoring other liabilities.

	STL + LTL	Shareholders' equity	D/E Ratio
FY 2020	99678	63078	1.58
FY 2019	90967	60179	1.51

BALANCE SHEET ANALYSIS

In the above case, a user should ascertain the reason for increase in shareholders' equity on YOY basis i.e., is it on account of retained earnings, fresh infusion of funds or something else. It should not be a case of retained earnings as company has incurred losses in FY 2019 as well as in FY 2020.

In this particular case it is the **foreign exchange translation gain** which have resulted into increase in the shareholder's equity.

In this particular case, the balance sheet is prepared in Rupee while the company has multicurrency exposure both in debt as well as in equity.

As a user of balance sheet, we need to be careful in interpreting the figures and comparing apple with apple only to arrive at any conclusion.

Efficiency Ratios

Efficiency ratios are used to understand, how effectively company is using its assets to generate income. These ratios are used to ascertain company's performance in short term.

Some of the common efficiency ratios are

- Inventory turnover ratio
- Account receivable turnover ratio
- Account payable turnover ratio
- Asset turnover ratio
- Day's sales in inventory

For working these ratios, analyst needs balance sheet as well as profit and loss statements. For the limited purpose of calculating these ratios we will use profit & loss statement also of the same public listed company whose balance sheet we have used above.

BALANCE SHEET ANALYSIS

			31 March 2020	31 March 2019
I.	Revenue from operations	33		
	(a) Revenue		258594.36	299190.59
	(b) Other Operating Revenues		2473.61	2747.81
	Total revenue from operations		**261067.97**	**301938.40**
II.	Other income (includes Government grants)	34	2973.15	2965.31
III.	Total Income (I+II)		**264041.12**	**304903.71**
IV.	Expenses			
	(a) Cost of materials consumed			
	(i) Cost of materials consumed		152968.74	182254.45
	(ii) Basis adjustment on hedge accounted derivatives		-297.27	-1245.37
	(b) Purchase of products for sale		12228.35	13258.83
	(c) Changes in inventories of finished goods, work-in-progress and products for sale		2231.19	2053.28
	(d) Employee benefits expense	35	30438.60	33243.87
	(e) Finance costs	36	7243.33	5758.60
	(f) Foreign exchange loss (net)		1738.74	905.91
	(g) Depreciation and amortisation expense		21425.43	23590.63
	(h) Product development/Engineering expenses		4188.49	4224.57
	(i) Other expenses	37	57087.46	62238.12
	(j) Amount transferred to capital and other account		-17503.40	-19659.59
	Total Expenses (IV)		**271749.66**	**306623.30**
V.	Profit/ (Loss) before exceptional items and tax (III-IV)		-7708.54	-1719.59
VI.	Exceptional Items			
	(a) Defined benefit pension plan amendment past service cost		-	147.90
	(b) Employee separation cost		436.14	1371.45
	(c) Provision/write off/(reversal)(net) of impairment of capital work-in-progress and intangibles under development (net)	47 (c)	-73.04	180.97
	(d) Provision for impairment of Passenger Vehicle Business	8 (a)	1418.64	-
	(e) Provision for Onerous Contracts	8 (b)	777.00	-
	(f) Provision/(reversal) for cost of closure of operation of a subsidiary		-65.62	381.01
	(g) Provision for impairment in subsidiary A	7	-	27837.91
	(h) Provision for impairment in other subsidiaries	47 (b)	353.20	-
	(i) Profit on sale of investment in a subsidiary Company		-	-376.08
	(j) Provision for loan given to a Joint venture		25.12	-
	(k) Others		-	109.27
VII.	Profit/(Loss) before tax (V-VI)		**-10579.98**	**-31371.15**
VIII.	Tax expense/(credit) (net):	22		
	(a) Current tax (including Minimum Alternate Tax)		1893.05	2225.23
	(b) Deferred tax		-1497.80	-4662.68
	Total tax expense/(credit) (net)		**395.25**	**-2437.45**
IX.	Profit/(loss) for the year from continuing operations (VII-VIII)		-10975.23	-28933.70
X.	Share of profit/(loss) of joint ventures and associates (net)	9	-1000.00	209.50
XI.	Profit/(loss) for the year (IX+X)		**-11975.23**	**-28724.20**

Inventory Turnover Ratio

Inventory turnover ratio indicates the rate at which a company sells and replaces its stock of goods in a given period. It measures companies' efficiency in selling its products / inventory. It enables the management to understand the optimum level of inventory required and thus reducing excess inventory purchase.

Inventory includes, raw material, work in process, finished unsold goods.

A higher inventory turnover ratio indicates good demand of product and thus bright prospects for the company. Against this a lower inventory turnover ratio indicates lower sales, higher stocks and weaker demand for company's products or inefficient marketing and distribution resulting in lower conversion of finished goods to sales.

The formula for calculating inventory turnover ratio is

$$\text{Inventory Turnover Ratio} = \frac{\text{Cost of Goods Sold}}{\text{Average Inventory}}$$

Cost of goods sold (COGS) includes the cost of raw material, direct labour cost and factory overheads used in manufacturing of the goods.

Average inventory is used to work out this ratio as inventory can be higher / lower at the time of preparation of balance sheet thus distorting the ratio. In case of non-availability of average inventory figures, the balance sheet figure can be taken.

In case cost of goods sold is not ascertainable, users can use total sales for arriving at inventory turnover ratio.

	Revenue	Inventory	Inv. Turn. Ratio
FY 2020	261067	37456	6.97
FY 2019	301938	39013	7.74

Only revenues directly connected with sales of goods needs to be taken into consideration.

This ratio indicates that company is able to rotate inventory approx. 7 times in FY 2020. This is an indication that company's products are in good demand and company commands a good position in the industry and thus able to sell its goods easily.

But before reaching above conclusion, we also need to compare this ratio with the industry average or peer groups.

Account receivable turnover ratio

Account receivable turnover ratio indicates the efficiency of a company in collection of its revenues. It calculates the number of times company is able to collect its average receivables in a period of time.

$$\text{Account Receivable Ratio} = \frac{\text{Net Credit Sales}}{\text{Average Account Receivable}}$$

In the sample profit and loss statement, the bifurcation of credit sales & cash sales is not given, so to work out account receivable turnover ratio, we are assuming that the entire sales are on credit basis.

	Sales	Account receivable	Ratio
FY 2020	261067	11172	23.37
FY 2019	301938	18996	15.89

The company's performance has improved in this parameter as the account receivables level has reduced much more in comparison to the reduction in sales.

An analyst should ask for bifurcation of sales between credit sales and cash sales to work out correct position of account receivable turnover ratio. Also, the average of account receivable level should be taken. This can be obtained by averaging the four quarters account receivable available in the quarterly balance sheet. Another and more common way to obtain average account receivables is to add the opening level of account receivables and closing level of account receivables and divide it by two.

From the above example, it is clear that the company has improved its efficiency in collection of receivables in FY. 2020 in comparison to FY. 2019. But please be careful as this ratio can be a misguiding one, as we have worked it out on the basis of closing balances and not the average balance of account receivables.

Also, we don't have bifurcation of credit sales and cash sales and we are going by an assumption that entire sales are credit sales.

Another aspect to be taken care while working out this ratio is to subtract the returns (sold items returned back by customers) from the credit sales to arrive at actual credit sales.

A high account receivables ratio also indicates that

- Company's customers are having good financial discipline.
- Company is conservative in extending credit.
- Company has good collection mechanism in place.
- Demand for company's products is good.

Account payable turnover ratio

The account payable as the name suggest are the credit availed by company from its suppliers and thus account payable turnover ratio indicates the average number of times a company pays to its suppliers / creditors in a given period of time.

Both account receivable and account payable turnover ratios are also indicators of company's short term liquidity position.

Higher ratio indicates company's capability to meet its short-term financial obligation in time but a very high ratio also indicates that company is not able to leverage upon its position and is missing on the opportunity to get higher credit period and thus better utilization of money.

A low ratio indicates company might be facing liquidity crunch and is not in a position to pay back to its creditors on time.

The formula to calculate account payable ratio is

$$\text{Account Payable Ratio} = \frac{\text{Net Credit Purchase}}{\text{Average Account Payable}}$$

Net credit purchase data is generally not available in the profit & loss statement, thus normally analyst use cost of goods sold + closing level of inventory-opening level of inventory to get the numerator.

To get the denominator the opening + closing level of account payable is divided by two.

Asset turnover ratio

Asset turnover ratio is used to ascertain the efficiency with which a company uses its assets to produce sales and generate revenue.

$$\text{Asset turnover ratio} = \frac{\text{Sales}}{\text{Total Assets}}$$

As can be seen from the ratio, the lower the assets & higher the sales, the better will be the ratio. Thus, a higher asset turnover ratio indicates efficient utilization of assets by company to generate higher sales.

This ratio varies from industry to industry as the inventory / assets requirement varies. Comparison between two companies in different sector will only misguide the user of balance sheet. Thus, this ratio should be used only for comparing companies in similar sector.

If a company is accumulating higher inventory / assets (may be for seasonal requirement) the ratio will get distorted.

The total assets in this ratio can be average of opening and closing level of assets in a financial year. Similarly, sales should be sales adjusted for returns (sales returned by customers).

Similar to asset turnover ratio in which we are using total assets, we can also work out **<u>fixed asset turnover</u>** ratio in which instead of total assets, only fixed assets are used and sales is divided by fixed assets to find the efficiency with which company is using its fixed assets to generate revenue.

Fixed assets are investment by company in plant and machinery and these have to be taken net of depreciation to work out fixed asset turnover ratio.

When a company acquires higher assets for future growth or dispose of assets, the ratio gets distorted, thus not reflecting true efficiency of the company.

	Sales	Total Asset	Ratio
FY 2020	261067	322121	0.81
FY 2019	301938	307194	0.98

** we are taking closing level of assets, but if past year balance sheets are available, please take average of opening & closing level of total assets.

We can see that in FY 2020 the ratio has worsen as the total assets have gone up at the same time the sales reduced. Thus, the performance of this company is worsening. But this ratio needs to be seen along with other ratios and industry average to get a true picture.

Day's sales of inventory

It is the number of days a company on an average takes to convert its inventory (including goods that are a work in process) to sales.

$$\text{Day's Sales of Inventory} = \frac{\text{Average Inventory}}{\text{Cost of Goods Sold}} \times 365$$

A high day's sales of inventory indicate inefficiency on the part of company to converts its inventory to sales. It might be because of number of reasons;

- Poor marketing efforts
- Higher accumulation of inventory
- Poor sales
- Low demand for company's goods
- Poor credit terms
- Bad pricing

Apart from a credit provider, there is another set of users of balance sheet known as investors. In next chapter, we will discuss the analysis of balance sheet from the perspective of an investor.

******

Sonu an investor

Sonu is new to stock market and has recently opened a demat & trading account with a stock broker. He started his trade by buying a random stock and was luck to book profit in his first intraday trade. He was very happy and thought trading intraday is the best strategy and started trading aggressively in intraday trade.

After a month he calculated his net profit and loss and was shocked to see that he has paid much more to his broker as brokerage + stamp duty etc., than the actual gains he has made in intraday trades.

He recalled, how much risks he has taken in these trades to book such a small profit. He decided to try some other method which can be less risky. He is well aware that stock market is a risky business but he is determined to find ways to reduce the risk.

He decided to get some knowledge on stock market and then to start again. He has heard about value investing and the benefits of value investing.

He read various books to familiarise himself with the concept of value investing. After reading these books, now he is confident that value investing is the way forward but the question arises how to find a stock worthy enough for investing.

He now understands that for value investing he needs to:

1. Understand financial statements

- Balance Sheet
- Profit & Loss Statement

- Cash Flow Statement
- Shareholding pattern
- Auditors' reports
- Management commentary in annual reports on growth prospects

1. Compay's fundamental growth aspects.
2. General economic and industry scenarios
3. Understanding of company's management
4. Ratio analysis

He took help of Ramu & Monu to understand basics of balance sheet and now is ready to move a step further in identifying value stocks.

He decided to compare stocks of different companies in similar industry by dividing their earning by number of shares outstanding to get per share earnings of the company. This is commonly known as **Earnings per Share** (EPS).

He observed that EPS is good but it is not giving the complete picture as a company with a smaller number of outstanding common shares is generating very high EPS in comparison to company with higher number of outstanding common shares, though the profit of first company is less in comparison to second company, thus it cannot be treated as a reflection of future growth potential of the company's stock.

He has seen a stock trading in the market at X price and was curious to know is it the true price or is this stock overvalued or undervalued in comparison to its balance sheet price.

He thought of finding the value of company's common share using balance sheet and with this thought he divided the total equity (asset-liability) by total number of outstanding common shares. The result of this gave him a value known as **book value** of stock.

This the value which a shareholder is entitled to get at the time of liquidation of the company after meeting all the other liabilities.

He found book value of stock to be an attractive concept and decided to use this concept to find if a stock is undervalued or overvalued.

But when he tried this method, he was not able to get many quality stocks trading near to book value. Most of the stocks are trading at multiple times to the book value.

To improvise from this basic concept, he divided the current market price of a stock by its book value. He has improvised on the book value concept to get a greater number of stocks which are not available near to book value but have a strong potential for future growth and are still available at very attractive price in comparison to their peer group or similar industry stocks.

Using this **Price / Book Value** concept, Sonu is now able to compare different stocks in the similar industry and is able to find some more quality stocks available at relatively cheaper price.

With the passage of time, Sonu is becoming smart and now he gets to know that other than the appreciation in stock price, he can also earn by way of a part of income which is distributed by company to its shareholder out of the profits earned by the company. This income distribution to shareholders out of profits is known as **dividends.**

Sonu has now got another tool to find attractive companies which can add value to his investment by distributing dividends. To compare various companies' dividend payment standards, he divided the dividend paid by a company in a year by its yearly net income. By doing this Sonu is able to get companies with regular and high **dividend payment ratio.**

He now decided to move on to another level of finding value stocks and for this he divided the current market price of share by the earnings per share. This ratio is known as **P/E Ratio.**

By doing this he got additional tool to compare different companies in an industry for finding hidden gems which are trading at lower than average of the price multiple of its earnings in a particular industry. This ratio gives an idea of number of years it will take for investor to get back his investment at a stable growth rate.

In this process, he realized that there are some very good companies available at very higher P/E ratio. These companies were having higher level of earnings growth in comparison to other companies available at lower P/E ratio. This leads him to come out with another ratio by dividing P/E ratio by EPS growth rate. This ratio considers growth also into calculation and thus enables user to find companies available at attractive price after taking growth rate into consideration. This ratio is known as **PEG ratio.**

******

Analysis of balance sheet-Investor

An intelligent investor will look for investing in a company which has potential to grow and is available at an attractive level.

Whether a company's present share price is attractive or not can be ascertained by analysing the balance sheet of the company and working out various financial ratio. We also need to use profit and loss statement for working out some of the key ratios used by investors.

Before we discuss the importance of valuation ratios, it needs to be understood that financial ratios are only one tool in analyzing the company's financial performance and future prospects. Along with ratio analysis, an investor also needs to look into various other aspects like, management efficiency, corporate governance, growth prospect of economy in general, growth prospects of the sector to which company represents etc.

Apart from ratios such as debt to equity ratio discussed above, some of the other key ratios used by investors are

- Earnings per share
- Book value
- Price / Book Value
- Return on Equity
- PE Ratio
- Dividend pay-out ratio
- Margin of Safety
- Price Earning to Growth

Earnings per share

Earnings per share is one of the key financial indicators used by fundamental investors in finding stocks for value investing.

Basic EPS and diluted EPS are used to measure the profitability of a company.

Basic EPS

Basic EPS, takes into account the company's outstanding common equity shares while diluted EPS includes employee stock options, warrants, convertible debts (bonds) which can be converted to equity or common stocks.

In case of convertible securities, new shares are issued, thus the number of shares increases, resulting in reduction of EPS.

As the number of shares are increasing on account of inclusion of convertible stocks, the dilution of EPS takes place and thus it's called diluted EPS.

It measures the earnings of company on per share basis.

This can be a very useful metrics to compare different companies' performances from the investors point of view.

$$EPS = \frac{\text{Net Income} - \text{Preferred Stock Dividends}}{\text{Average Outstanding Shares}}$$

Preferred stock dividends are dividends which though are not guaranteed but get priority over common stock dividends.

	No of Shares O/S (in cr.)	Net Income (in crore)	Basic EPS
FY 2020	359.74	-12070	-33.55
FY 2019	339.58	-18826	-84.88

In this case as the company is loss making, thus EPS is in negative. An investor generally looks for higher EPS.

In case of early stages of a company the income will be low, in such cases the EPS will be either very low or negative. An investor needs to look beyond EPS to understand the value in the company to take an investment decision.

Diluted EPS

In case of diluted EPS, it is assumed that all convertible securities are converted to equity i.e., the right by security holder to convert the securities to equity is exercised.

$$\text{Diluted EPS} = \frac{\text{Net Income - Preferred Stock Dividends}}{\text{Average Outstanding Shares + dilutive Shares}}$$

Diluted EPS can also be treated as a worst-case scenario when all the convertible securities are converted to equity thus impacting the earning per share of the company.

As in case of diluted EPS the denominator is increasing without having any impact on the numerator, thus the diluted EPS will be lower than basic EPS in cases where company has convertible securities, else the diluted EPS will be equal to basic EPS.

Cash EPS

For working cash EPS, non-cash expenses like depreciation are added back to the net profit & loss to arrive at net income. It is the operating cash flow of the company divided by the number of outstanding shares.

$$\text{Cash EPS} = \frac{\text{Operating Cash Flow}}{\text{Diluted Outstanding Shares}}$$

	No of Shares O/S (in cr.)	Net Income + Depreciation (in cr.)	Cash EPS
FY 2020	359.74	10450	29.04
FY 2019	339.58	-5343	-15.73

A company with higher cash EPS is assumed to have better capability to generate cash flow and thus better financial performance.

Cash EPS is less prone to accounting manipulation and thus is a useful tool for comparison.

Now the question arises, which EPS is good?

The answer to this question is, each EPS serves its purpose and a user of balance sheet needs to take care to use similar metrics to compare financial performance of different companies or a company's historic performance.

Book Value

Book value is the net assets value of a firm. The equation for arriving book value is

Book Value = Total Assets – Total Liabilities

We also know that Total assets- Total Liabilities = Net Worth

Thus, we can assume that

Book value = Net Worth

Net worth = Shareholder's equity + Retained Earning

This is the amount which investors are entitled to get in case of liquidation of a company after meeting its liabilities.

Book value of an asset is the original purchase price of asset – accumulated depreciation.

Book value per share

Book value per share is calculated by subtracting all debt, liabilities and the liquidation price of preferred stock from the company's total assets and then dividing the value arrived by number of outstanding shares of common stock.

$$BVPS = \frac{\text{Total Shareholder's equity - preferred equity}}{\text{Total outstanding common shares}}$$

> Value investor will always look for shares of company's trading near to their book values or below their book value. The more the share price of a company is trading close to or below the book value, the greater will be the safety of principal (subject to other fundamental aspects).

Legendary investors like Benjamin Graham, Warren Buffett have used this as a key part of their investment strategy to build fortunes.

An inflated assets will inflate the net worth, which in turn inflate the book value per share. Thus, it makes job of a prudent investor more difficult. An investor should not be guided only by the balance sheet figures of shareholders equity value but also use the accounting concepts as advised in International Accounting Standards to ascertain the correctness in classification of assets and liabilities in the balance sheet.

Particularly in case of unlisted companies it becomes challenging to find the exact book value per share.

When book value per share exceeds the market value of the share, the stock is deemed as undervalued.

The book value per share can be increased by either reducing the average outstanding common stocks or by increasing net assets.

Companies repurchases their stocks to reduce the average outstanding shares and thus improving the book value per share.

The second way is by keeping the liabilities at the lower side and increasing the net assets, thus increasing the net worth.

In case of asset light companies like software companies which generally have very low value of assets, the book value will be very low. Thus, comparing book values of companies in different sector will not give proper results and thus and investor should compare book values of companies in similar sector only.

Before using book value to use as a tool for investment, an investor should also ascertain reasons for the company's stock trading below its book value. The probable reason could be

- Lack of investor's confidence
- Fundamentally weak company
- Loss making company
- Inflated net worth by use of creative accounting.

A company will have negative book value when, company has higher liabilities in comparison to assets, thus indicating financial weakness and balance sheet insolvency.

	Shareholders' Equity	Shares O/S	BVPS
FY 2020	63078	359.74	175.34
FY 2019	60179	339.58	177.21

Tangible Book Value Per Share

In case of BVPS, we have used formula Total Assets- Liabilities to work out the Net worth or Shareholder's equity, but the total assets also include intangible assets like goodwill, patents, etc., and in times of liquidation, it generally becomes very difficult to realize the book value of intangible assets to the fullest extent.

To overcome above challenge a more refined formula for calculating BVPS could be TBVPS i.e., tangible book value per share.

In TBVPS, we will exclude intangible assets from the total assets to work out the shareholders equity.

	Total Assets - Intangibles	Total Liabilities	equity
FY 2020	252926	258229	-5302
FY 2019	245982	246491	-509

It can be seen that the shareholder's equity turned negative when we have considered only tangible assets for calculating book value per share and the interpretation of balance sheet for an investor will now be different.

The TBVPS will also be in negative and can be obtained by dividing Shareholder's equity by average number of outstanding shares.

So, in analysis of balance sheet, we need to understand the importance of each and every item in the balance sheet and a correct interpretation can only lead us to positive outcome.

It is not the case that intangible assets are always to be discounted, an investor needs to take a call on value generated by intangible assets and the likely value it will continue to generate even in case of difficulties.

In the above example of the listed company's balance sheet and also in case of IT companies, the intangible assets i.e., brand value, patents are of significant importance and thus it will be wrong to get guided by TBVPS instead of BVPS.

Price to Book Ratio

Price to book ratio is used to compare companies market capitalization to its book value thus, reflecting the company's net assets available to common shareholders relative to the market price of its stock.

$$P/B \text{ Ratio} = \frac{\text{Market Price Per Share}}{\text{Book Value Per Share}}$$

A ratio higher than one, indicates the market is willing to pay higher price for the company's shares than its net asset price.

A company with less than one P/B ratio indicates, investors are unwilling to pay a price higher than the book price. The reason could be lack of confidence by investors on the fundamental growth prospects of the company.

A high growth company will generally have P/B ratio way above one while a financially distressed company will generally have P/B ratio below one.

The interpretation of lower P/B ratio by a value investor can be different. A company with lower P/B value ratio is an opportunity subject to the fundamental position & growth prospects of company being strong. A value investor will look for fundamentally strong company with P/B ratio less than one or lower than the industry average.

An investor should not discard a company if its P/B ratio is less than one, in fact, he should go deep into the company's financials, its management, its growth prospects, industry scenario, past record, news related to company and then only should decide on whether to invest or leave the stock.

Market value of share are generally higher than the book value and thus it's an opportunity if investor is getting a share of a fundamentally strong company at the book value or lower than the book value.

The basic difference in Market Value and Book Value is market value is forward looking value of company's equity and thus reflects company's growth prospects while book value is based on historic data.

There is no specific P/B ratio which can be treated as good or bad, an investor needs to compare the industry ratio with the company's ratio to ascertain if the share is available at decent price or not. A good P/B ratio for one industry can be bad for another industry, thus comparing companies in similar sector is important.

Return on Equity

Return on equity is a tool in fundamental analysis of balance sheet and used to find out percentage of return generated by a company over its equity. It is used to compare companies in similar industry and to find out companies generating better returns on equity. Companies generating higher return on equity can be attractive for investors.

$$\text{ROE} = \frac{\text{Net Income}}{\text{Average shareholder's equity}}$$

Net income is the income after netting off expenses and taxes paid during a given period.

Further for calculating ROE the net income is arrived after dividends paid to preferred shareholders & interest paid to lenders but before allocation of dividends to common shareholders.

ROE is a useful tool in evaluating investment returns. An investor can compare industry average ROE to the company's ROE to form a view on the profit generating capability of the targeted company.

A company with ROE higher than the industry average or peer group will be the preferred company for investors. ROE gives an insight into the effective use of shareholders capital for generating returns by company's management.

An investor needs to ascertain the historical trend in ROE. A sustainable and increasing ROE over time indicates company to be a worthy investment option. While an irregular and decreasing ROE indicates financial troubles and investors generally do not give such company preference over other steady ROE generating company because a decreasing ROE indicates that management is not able to use investor money properly or are using money in non-productive assets.

A user of balance sheet needs to be careful in arriving at conclusion on the basis of ROE. A very high ROE can be on account of very low shareholder's equity. It indicates that the promoter's stake is very low in a company and thus company can be prone to risk as promoters will lose interest as soon as the company lend in some financial trouble because promoters don't have much at risk.

Further it can also indicate that the company is using very high debt in comparison to equity to fund its business, resulting in higher leverage. A very high leverage is generally negative for an investor.

Similarly, a company in the initial period of operations or project under implementation can have very low ROE as the returns generated will be small in comparison to the equity investment.

Another case for very high ROE could be a company incurring loss in the previous year's thus eroding its capital and then a sudden profit on account of higher business, accounting change or tax returns etc can inflate the ratio as the denominator has reduced.

To overcome this, investors need to compare past trends, industry average or peer group average.

Further investor also needs to take care that the company is in profit and its net shareholders equity is also in positive because a negative income and negative shareholder equity can also give positive ROE.

BALANCE SHEET ANALYSIS

The multiplying effect of leverage on ROE can be understood by following equation

$$\text{ROE} = \frac{\text{Net Income}}{\text{Total Asset}} \times \frac{\text{Total Assets}}{\text{Equity}}$$

$$\text{ROE} = \text{ROA} \times \text{Leverage}$$

Price to earnings Ratio

Price to earnings ratio compares market price of share with the earning per share & is one of the most common tools used by investors in identifying potential stocks for investment.

This ratio is also known as **price multiple** or **earning multiple** as it shows the number of times market price of a share is to its earning per share.

A high P/E ratio indicates either the company is overvalued or the market is optimistic about the future growth prospects of the company and thus willing to pay higher money.

$$P/E\ Ratio\ =\ \frac{Market\ Price\ per\ Share}{Earnings\ per\ Share}$$

At constant earnings, P/E ratio also indicates the number of years a company will require to pay back the amount invested.

A standalone P/E ratio will be of no use. An investor needs to compare P/E ratio of a company with its own historical P/E ratio as well as peer group of companies in the similar industry to have a comparative understanding of where the company is heading and how worthy is it to invest at present market price.

From the above data, it looks like that Oracle with the lowest P/E ratio can be a good investment and PayPal with highest P/E ratio and lowest EPS can be avoided by investors as the valuations are very high in comparison to earnings.

But this should not be the only reason to invest in Oracle and avoiding other stocks, for reaching any conclusion, we also need to see the earnings per share which is also 2nd lowest in case of Oracle thus indicating that company's income generating capacity is lower in comparison to other major players thus growth prospects could not be that encouraging.

While investing in a stock it is important to also look at other growth prospects of the company and also the past trend.

Company	P/E Ratio	EPS
Microsoft	37.75	7.41
Google	33.30	75.93
Facebook	29.57	11.84
Oracle	18.71	4.70
PayPal	67.24	4.45

The historic P/E ratios of Oracle are as under

Company	2017	2018	2019	2020
Oracle	51.91	17.04	17.48	17.31
PayPal	50.08	49.18	52.26	66.16

From above table, it is clear that Oracle's P/E ratio has come down in 2018. Now as a prudent investor, you need to find out the reasons for fall in P/E.

Let's find out the Basic EPS for both the companies

Company	2017	2018	2019	2020
Oracle	0.87	3.05	3.16	4.67
PayPal	1.49	1.74	2.09	3.58

From above data, we can ascertain that Oracle is a better choice for value investing in comparison to PayPal subject to other fundamental being on similar lines.

Dividend Payout Ratio

Dividend payout ratio is the ratio of dividend paid out to the shareholders out of the total net income of the company. Dividend is paid out of profits and if a company is in loss than question of payment of dividend does not arises.

Companies are not under compulsion to pay dividend; they can retain a part or full profit for future expansion of business and growth.

Many investors invest in stocks of companies having a history of paying consistent dividend. Apart from increase in the share price of a stock, dividend adds up to the gains for the shareholders.

The dividend paid also compensate to certain extend for the fall in prices of stocks.

An investor expects companies not paying dividend and retaining profits to generate higher return by way of increase in share price.

A conservative prudent investor will prefer stocks with consistent dividend payout history over other stocks. An investor has to find a balance between dividend paying stocks and growth stocks.

Growth stocks are generally stocks of companies which are in growth stage and thus use the retained profits for subsequent growth of company, thus not paying divided or paying divided at a low rate.

But stocks price of such companies generally rises much faster and thus compensating the loss on account on non-payment of dividend.

Regular payment of dividend indicates ethical management practice as dividend is a right of shareholder. Shareholder has invested in the company with the intention to receive dividend and if a company persistently choose not to pay dividend than it is not doing justice with the shareholders rights.

The dividend payout ratio indicates, how much company is paying to its shareholders and how much it is retaining for future growth, debt payment etc.

$$\text{Dividend Payout Ratio} = \frac{\text{Dividend Paid}}{\text{Net Income}}$$

Retention Ratio = 1- Dividend Payout Ratio

It can also be defined in terms of per share ratio

$$\text{Retention Ratio} = \frac{\text{EPS-DPS}}{\text{EPS}}$$

EPS = Earnings per share & DPS = Dividend per share

Dividend payout ratio is also industry specific and a user of balance sheet should compare companies in the similar sector only for better comparison.

Real Estate Investment Trust or Infrastructure Investment Trust are under obligation to distribute 90% of profit generated in a given financial years as dividend thus cannot be compared with other sectors.

A very high dividend payout can also be negative for the investor. It might indicate that company is hiding something from the investor and to divert their attention paying higher dividend.

It can also indicate that the company is not focusing on future growth and not investing the profit generated for further improvement of business. Thus, there has to be a fine balance between retention and dividend payment.

An investor should look for regular dividend paying companies. Consistency is more important than a one-off large dividend payment.

For comparing companies having different share price, dividend yield can be a better metrics.

$$\text{Dividend Yield} = \frac{\text{Dividend per share}}{\text{Price per share}}$$

Margin of Safety

Margin of safety is a concept in which investor invest in stocks only when they are available at a significant discount to their intrinsic value. The thought is that downside risk will be lower in such stocks and upside potential is higher.

Margin of safety does not guarantee good returns or protection against loss of principal but if done along with fundamental analysis can to a greater extend will reduce the chances of incurring significant losses.

For finding a stock with higher margin of safety, an investor should be in a position to work out the intrinsic value of the stock

Watch out for stocks which are fundamentally strong but are trading below the average price of its peer group of stocks or are trading below their book value. For this an investor can use P/E ratio, P/B ratio etc.

For an investor, who is not very comfortable in using the formulas, he can simply watch for stocks which have fallen significantly but are fundamentally strong and are falling because of some temporary event. These can be a good target for value investing. But be careful in understanding the reason for such fall and should invest in the company only if the fall is not attributed to fundamental weakness.

In such cases systematic purchase can be a good option as no one knows to which level the stock will fall, thus purchasing through a SIP will reduce the risk and give average price for the investment.

Also, an investor needs to have patience to resist from jumping to take position when a stock is falling and should understand the causes for such fall.

If the broader market is falling than any stock will fall but that gives an opportunity to value investors to accumulate quality stocks at attractive prices.

In any case, a value investor should shy away from stocks which are fundamentally weak or are overvalued as margin for safety will generally be very low.

You can also refer to book "The Intelligent Investor" written by Benjamin Graham in which he has suggested a mathematical formula for finding out intrinsic value of a stock.

Price / Earnings to Growth Ratio

PEG ratio is a modified version of P/E ratio and includes EPS growth rate also into calculation.

PEG Ratio	=	$\dfrac{\text{Price / EPS}}{\text{EPS Growth}}$

The PEG ratio takes into account the EPS growth expected in the future. As this ratio is also taking into account growth rate, it can be a more useful ratio than P/E ratio for comparison of stocks.

This ratio apart from historical values also depends upon future growth estimates for the next 1-3 years or more and thus it is vulnerable to individual analyst estimations.

Historic EPS

Company	2017	2018	2019	2020	2021
Microsoft	3.29	2.15	5.11	5.82	7.41
Google	18.27	44.22	49.59	63.45	75.93
Facebook	5.49	7.65	6.48	10.22	11.84
Oracle	0.87	3.05	3.16	4.67	4.70
PayPal	1.49	1.74	2.09	3.58	4.45

Estimated EPS

For the purpose of understanding calculations, let's assume the average growth in EPS is going to continue in future. For calculating average EPS growth, we have removed the figures which are significantly away from mean and arrived at the average of the remaining figures.

Company	P/E Ratio	2022 (EPS growth rate estimation.)	PEG
Microsoft	37.75	20.61%	183.16
Google	33.30	19.92%	167.17
Facebook	29.57	37.64%	78.56
Oracle	18.71	2.12%	882.55
PayPal	67.24	20.40%	329.61

If we compare P/E ratio than oracle seems to be the cheapest stock but when we include growth rate of EPS also into consideration than despite of a higher P/E ratio, Facebook becomes attractive choice with lowest PEG and actually can be cheaper than Oracle.

So, while choosing stock, only looking at P/E ratio will not serve the purpose and an investor also needs to consider the future growth rate of the company to find an attractive stock.

A value investor prefers a stock with low P/E ratio. A stock having valuation much below its intrinsic value. As against this a growth-oriented investor will prefer higher P/E ratio company and believes that the higher earnings growth justifies higher P/E Ratio.

Market generally looks for forward P/E ratio and for calculating forward P/E ratio the EPS projections are taken into consideration.

BALANCE SHEET ANALYSIS

******

About the author

Raj Kumar Sharma, a banker by profession and writer by choice, has experience in different segment of banking and finance. Grown up in a modest town of central India, Bhopal, Raj Kumar has completed his graduation from Bhopal University.

He got inspiration to write book's during his stint as a trainer in one of the prestigious training institute of a leading bank in India. The Eureka moment came when his work got recognition in competitions organized by National Institute of Bank Management-Pune & Indian Institute of Banking & Finance. He likes to write on both fiction and non-fiction topics.

His first book was a self-help book with the title " My Choice, My Life". In this book he has discussed the impact of the choices one makes in his day-to-day affairs.

Being a banker by profession, his second book was on a banking related topic that is "Ratio Analysis". This book in on the importance of key financial ratio and their uses.

His third book " Export Business-A Beginner's Guide" is a guide inspired by make in India initiative for young generation entrepreneurs & guide them to start their export business.

His fourth book "Destination-Beyond Frontiers" is a science fiction novel taking its readers to adventures journey into the unknown space.

****

Other books by the author

<u>Ratio Analysis</u>

Ratio Analysis is an integral part of the assessment of the financial position of an organization. By analyzing ratios one can get a fair idea about the health of the organization. Ratio analysis gives an insight into the operational efficiency, liquidity, leverage, solvency & profitability of the organization. This book briefs about the key financial ratios & their importance in decision-making. These ratios are important not only in providing any debt support to the company but also in taking a decision to invest in the shares of the company. For any investor who wishes to learn fundamental analysis of stocks, this book is a first step towards the same.

<u>Export Business- A Beginner's Guide</u>

Many of us have somewhere deep in our heart a wish to become an entrepreneur. Due to unavailability of right information, many of us were unable to venture into this promising segment of international trade and remained confined to meeting our day-to-day needs.

This book is an attempt to bring the much-needed information in one place to enable a prospective entrepreneur to venture into international trade. This book tries to bridge the crucial knowledge gap and provide information on areas related to international trade.

This book enables the prospective entrepreneurs to have a know-how of legal requirements, the way to find market & buyers, the requirement of different countries the risk involved, and the risk mitigation measures, the documentation, and the process involved.

My Choice My Life

This book is based on small day-to-day events which occur in a common human being's life and how we can learn from these incidences to re-shape our way of conducting ourselves and to improve upon. In any situation, we will have more than one way to react to the situation and if we give ourselves a little time then we can realize immediately which way is the right one.

Destination-Beyond Frontiers

A science fiction novel taking its readers to the adventurous journey into the unknown space. A work of fiction inspired by discoveries and inventions by humans.

******

Declaration

Contents of this book have nothing to do with organization author works for and views and ideas expressed in the book were author's personal view.